Santander
Castro-Urdiales
Bilbao
Gernika
San Sebastián
Irún
Pto. Roncesvalles
Pto. Somport
Pamplona
Jaca
Carrión de los Condes
Fromista
Castrojeriz
Burgos
San Juan de Ortega
Santo Domingo de la Calzada
Nájera
Logroño
Estella
Puente la Reina

In the same collection:

Wow, the Stone Age!

# The Flying Pilgrim

Lawrence Schimel / Sara Rojo

EDICIONES
Aldeasa

On a clear morning, a swallow flew in lazy figure eights among the **spires** of the Cathedral of Santiago, before settling on one elaborate cornice to rest and admire the view over the entire city and the countryside beyond. She watched the constant streams of humans entering the city on foot or on bicycle, instead of only in cars as they did the rest of the year.

"What a curious **migration** pattern," the swallow said to herself. "I wonder where they all come from?"

The swallow launched herself into the air and glided down to the railing of the steps of the **Obradoiro Façade** to get a better look. She watched curiously as the humans filed into the Cathedral. Most looked up at the ceiling as soon as they entered the door. Many paused to touch the **Portico de la Gloria** as they passed it, some of them sticking their fingers into the crevices in the marble, like they were digging into bark for a bug. But when they pulled their hands free, they were empty. Some reached out to knock three times on the head of one of the figures carved on the **column of the Parteluz**. The swallow had no idea why they did any of these things. But then, who could explain the strange actions of humans, anyway?

"Don't you think there are more of them this year than last?" the swallow asked of a plump pigeon who was perched nearby.

"Does it matter? I hadn't noticed," the pigeon said.

The swallow had hoped that her fellow **avian** would be able to enlighten her. So she tried again.

"Where do they all come from? I sometimes wonder if I should fly overhead and find out."

"Why go to them, when they'll come to us?" the pigeon replied. "And they bring food with them. Look at that bit of bread the one dressed in red just dropped." And with that, the pigeon flew off to claim its snack before another bird did.

The swallow was disappointed by the pigeon's lack of curiosity. But what could one expect of a bird who ate crumbs instead of insects, after all?

As she watched more and more humans entering the Cathedral, the swallow's curiosity only increased. Where did all these humans come from, and why more this year than previous years? What did they do here? And where did they all go? Because while there were constant streams of humans walking or bicycling into the city, they did not leave the same way.

Maybe a creature that walks instead of flies will know the answers, the swallow thought. Taking to the air once again, the swallow spied a dog in the Plaza Quintana on the opposite side of the Cathedral. Dogs were not as dangerous as cats, but just in case, the swallow landed on the steps that divided the upper part of the plaza from the lower area, where the dog and his master were. The dog's owner was busy taking photographs of the other door, the one surround by all sorts of sculptures of humans. The swallow was certain it hadn't been opened the year before or the year before that, but ever since this past winter it hadn't been closed, no matter what the weather was.

"Do you know where all the humans come from?" the swallow asked the dog.
"I'm not sure," the dog answered. "All I know is that they all smell like far away."

Well, the swallow decided, since neither the creatures who fly through the air nor those who walk on the ground can help me, I'm just going to have to find out for myself.

As she soared over the city again looking down, the swallow could see that the humans arrived from all directions! Which trail of them should she follow?

It seemed that more humans came from the east, where the sun rose in the morning, than any other direction. So the swallow decided that that was the path she would follow.

There were fewer humans on the road in the early afternoon than there had been in the morning. But the swallow was not to be deterred. Filled with enthusiasm to finally be doing something to find out the answers to these questions that had haunted her, she flew on despite the summer heat. She was on an adventure!

Hours passed and the swallow flew and flew, following the road the humans walked or rode to get to Santiago. Soon, the swallow had flown further away from the city than she had ever been before in her life. Would she be able to find his way home again? she wondered. But then she laughed. "How could I get lost?" she said to herself. "I can just follow the humans who are all walking there. But first, I want to solve the mystery of why they go there."

The swallow was not used to flying so much in one day and her wings began to ache from the effort. She stopped to rest more and more frequently, but each time she pushed herself to continue her journey and find the answers she sought. Soon the swallow realized she would need to find someplace to sleep. Where could she stay that would be safe from **predators**? What did the humans do who were walking here? They did not carry homes with them...

At last, she saw some walkers below who turned off the road and entered a building. Maybe I can find sanctuary here as well, the swallow thought. She slipped inside the refuge through a window left open to let in the breeze. To her surprise, the floor was covered with sleeping humans! It looked almost like a living carpet. What a curious building, the swallow thought. She had never seen anything like it.

The swallow was too exhausted from flying to try and discover more. Tomorrow, she told herself, and settled herself on a windowsill, where she would be safe from cats or other animals. The swallow had closed her eyes already, but just before she fell asleep she overheard a young human tell a larger one, "Mommy, my feet hurt from walking. Will we have to walk home?"

The mother answered, "We're almost there, honey. And don't worry. We'll fly home, so you can rest."
"So you can rest!" the swallow thought, as she stretched her aching wings one last time before falling asleep. "As if flying were restful! How ridiculous!"

The next day, the swallow woke with the dawn. Many of the humans also woke at that time, even though in the city the swallow had seen many humans who stayed asleep until much later.

She stretched her sore wings, and observed that many humans likewise stretched themselves in preparation for the day's walking.

The swallow wanted to stay and try to overhear more of their conversations, but she was hungry for breakfast and flew outside to find something to eat. When she flew back to the building, her stomach now full, she saw that many of the humans had already started walking toward Santiago de Compostela. Well, the swallow decided, I'll just have to keep on with my journey and try to find the next batch of travelers. Maybe they will reveal the secrets of where they all come from, and why!

Once again, the swallow settled in to a long flight, heading down the road away from Santiago de Compostela, in search of the answers to her questions.

As the morning passed, the swallow saw a small spire poking up above the trees ahead of her. It reminded her of the spires of the Cathedral where she liked to rest, and so she flew closer to investigate. It was a small church, and just as the swallow approached she saw a tiny church mouse emerge from the door.

The swallow landed on a branch of a nearby tree.
"Good morning, mouse," she called down.
The mouse politely answered, "Good morning, swallow. You haven't seen a cat hiding hereabouts, as you were flying in?"
"No, thankfully I did not," the swallow answered. "And if I can ask a question of my own. Do you know why so many humans go walking toward Santiago de Compostela in the summer?"
"Of course," the mouse answered. "I've overheard the priest talk about it. They're called *peregrinos*."
"Peregrines? But those are hawks not humans! And hawks are dangerous! They eat mice and birds and anything they can get their talons on!"
"They're not **peregrine hawks**, they're pilgrims. They're making a journey to visit the saint who's buried in the Cathedral."
"And where do they all come from?" the swallow asked.

But before the mouse had a chance to answer, a cat came racing around the corner of the building.
"Look out," the swallow shouted to her new friend, and the mouse disappeared inside.
The swallow was going to wait for the mouse to come out again so they could talk more, but the cat had settled down in front of the door to wait as well, and the swallow decided to continue her journey, taking to the skies once more.

As the day passed into afternoon, the swallow saw a group of humans paused beside a riverbank. She decided to stop for a rest as well, and maybe overhear their conversation. She took a drink from the river, and when she looked up again she saw some more humans had come along the road as well.

"Mind if we join you?" one of the new arrivals called out.
"We'd be delighted to share this bit of shade with our fellow pilgrims," came the reply from one of the group that had already been there.

The swallow flitted closer to make sure she could overhear their conversation.

"It's a relief to stop and rest a while," a newcomer said. "I'm glad we're almost there."
"Is this your first pilgrimage?" one of the others asked.
"Yes. How about for all of you?"
"We've done chunks of the pilgrimage before, but never the whole thing. But I'd promised the saint that if he helped my father get well from the cancer, I'd make the entire journey. Now here I am."
"Well," the newcomer said, "I'm glad that your father got well. I'm going for a much less meaningful reason, I guess. My name is Santiago, so I decided to see my **namesake**."
"Whyever you make the journey, the reason is valid," said one of the others who'd been resting by the riverbank.

It's no wonder no one could tell me why the humans walk to Santiago, the swallow thought. They each have their own reason for doing so!

The swallow listened as they told stories about their earlier days walking the Camino, or sometimes about short parts of the journey they had made in earlier years.

As the group was conversing, some more travelers appeared. "Hallo!" one called out.

"Hola," the group responded.

"They come from Germany," Santiago explained, "we met them a few days ago at one of the refuges. They don't speak much Spanish, but every day they learn some new words. Maybe if we all walk together, they can teach us some words in German, and we can teach them some words in Spanish, and the journey will pass the quicker."

"I think that's a wonderful idea. They must have such interesting stories to tell, having come from so far. We live in Pamplona, so one of the routes of the Camino passes right by us. But to have walked here from another country!"

When the humans had continued on their journey, the swallow stayed where she was by the riverside, thinking on all that she had learned. The humans came to Santiago de Compostela from many different places. Sometimes even from as far away as different countries.

And they came to Santiago for so many different reasons, sometimes religious and sometimes secular.

When she had first begun to wonder about the humans who came to her city, the swallow had never realized that the answers to her questions would be so complicated, with so many different shades of meaning!

The swallow was glad to have decided to set out herself in search of these answers, because even if her journey had left her with some new questions about the travelers, she felt satisfied by the knowledge it had given her.

That night, the swallow rested in a hollow of a tree, and in the morning she began the flight back to the city where she made her home.

She stopped again at the little church, flying all the way around it to make sure that the cat wasn't hiding behind the corners.
"It's safe to come out, mouse," the swallow said.

The tiny mouse poked its snout out the door.
"Hello again, traveler. Have you more questions to ask or have you already found the answers?"
"I think there will always be more questions to ask," the swallow said, "because each answer makes me curious about something else. But I did have one question you might be able to help me with. It seems to me that there are more people making the pilgrimage to Santiago de Compostela this year than last year. Do you know why?"
"Yes, I do know the answer to this because again I have heard the priest talk about it. This is a special Jubilee Year, because Santiago's feast day falls on a Sunday. So more people decide to walk the pilgrimage during the holy year, in honor of the Saint and to pay him homage.
The next Jubilee year won't be for eleven more years!"

The swallow thanked the mouse for his help, and continued her journey homeward.

As the swallow flew homeward toward Santiago de Compostela, she passed again the group of travelers she had seen by the riverside. They were walking along the road all together, as new friends, teaching one another their respective languages and telling stories of their homelands.

Flying over their heads along the road, the swallow realized that she, too, was following one of the many routes of the pilgrimage. "I wonder if that makes me a *peregrino*, too!" the swallow said aloud with a laugh. She imagined herself as a fierce peregrine hawk, causing terror to the little creatures below in her shadow. But the swallow decided she was happier as herself, and if she was a *peregrino* it was only as a pilgrim on a journey of knowledge.

**some words you did not know...**

### [Spire] page 4

An architectural term referring to a tall, acutely-pointed adornment on the top of a building, often representing the tallest point(s) of said building. Sometimes also called pinnacles.

### [Migration] page 4

The geographic movement of individuals or groups from one area to another. Many types of birds and other animals migrate to warmer regions during the cold Winter months, returning in Spring or Summer.

### [Obradoiro Façade] page 7

Façade is an Architectural term meaning the outside or "face" of a building. Built in the 18th century, the Obradoiro Façade is the Baroque front that covers the earlier Romanesque face the Cathedral used to wear. At the Plaza with the same name,it is the main entrance to the cathedral of Santiago through which pilgrims enter to see the Apostle.

### [Portico de la Gloria] page 7

Located inside the Obradoiro Façade, this portico was sculpted by Master Mateo with the figure of Christ, the Apostles and Prophets, a group of ancient musciand, and monsters of various forms.

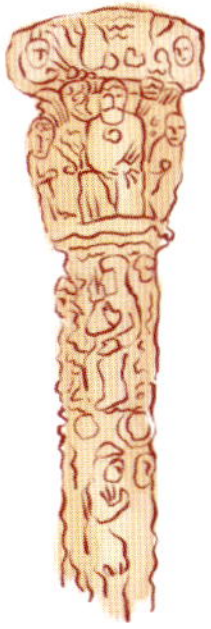

### [Columna del Parteluz] page 7

This column divides the Póritco de la Gloria. It is in the shape of a tree and some pilgrims stick their fingers in the holes among the branches, in the hopes of getting as many mercies as the number of fingers inserted. On the other side is the Santo dos Croques, a figure which is said to be a self-portrait of Master Mateo. Some pilgrims give him a rap on the head in hopes that his inspiration might be contagious or transferable.

### [Namesake] page 20

The person or Saint that someone was named after, as a sign of respect.

### [Avian] page 7

A bird, or relating to the world of birds.

### [Jubilee Year] page 24

When the Saint's day for the Apostle James falls on a Sunday, that year is known as a special Jubilee Year, and many faithful make a pilgrimage to Santiago to honor the Apostle and beg him for benedictions. A Jubilee year occurs every 5-6-5-11 years, then the cycle repeats.

### [Peregrine falcon] page 27

A raptor (that is, a predatory bird) that lives in wooded areas, in mountains with cliffs, and near certain cities.

### [Predator] page 12

An animal that hunts and devours animals of other species as the basis for its diet.

Coordination and production: **Ediciones Aldeasa**

Written by: **Lawrence Schimel**

Illustrated by: **Sara Rojo**

Graphic Design: **Carmen Olivares**

Layout: **Cromotex**

Repro: **Cromotex**

Printed by: **Artes gráficas Palermo, S.L.**



ISBN: 84-8003-908-6

Depósito Legal: M-18334-2004

# The Flying Pilgrim

Santiago de Compostela
Lavacolla
Lugo
Portomarín
O Cebreiro
Villafranca del Bierzo
Ponferrada
Astorga
Órbigo
León
Oviedo
Ribadesella
Sahagún